JOURNEY
TO THE
STARS

KALPANA CHAWLA, ASTRONAUT

by **Laurie Wallmark** and **Raakhee Mirchandani**

illustrated by **Maitreyi Ghosh**

beaming ☀ **books**
MINNEAPOLIS

As a young girl, Kalpana liked to climb to the roof of her house and wonder at the skies. When small planes flew overhead, she waved to the pilots.

Kalpana begged her father to take her to the local flying club. When she was eleven, he finally agreed, and she took her first airplane ride. After that, she was hooked.

In drawing class at school, she sketched airplanes instead of landscapes. For a science project, Kalpana charted the sky and constellations. At night, she gazed at the stars, dreaming of flying and going into space.

At age fourteen, Kalpana decided she wanted to become an aeronautical engineer—so she could build aircrafts. After finishing grade twelve, Kalpana attended a local college. Since they didn't offer enough engineering courses, she transferred to Punjab Engineering College.

Here, the faculty tried to discourage her interest in aeronautical engineering. But Kalpana knew what she wanted. She wouldn't let others tell her what to do.

In 1982, Kalpana became the first woman to graduate with a degree in aeronautical engineering from her college. Diploma in hand, she decided to attend the University of Texas at Arlington, far away from her home and family in India. Kalpana was going to continue her studies and chase her dreams. Since she was such a good student, the university even provided money to help her pay for school.

On her second day in Texas, Kalpana met Jean-Pierre "JP" Harrison, a flight instructor. He shared her love for flying. They discussed airplanes for hours on end.

Kalpana's dreams were starting to take flight!

Kalpana and JP also enjoyed spending time in nature and would go hiking and scuba diving, and JP often flew them in a small two-seater plane to explore new places. They soon fell in love. A year later, the two married.

After earning her master's degree, Kalpana went on
to receive a PhD in aeronautical engineering from the
University of Colorado Boulder.

Kalpana took flying lessons and earned her own pilot's license. Since she was short, she had to sit on a cushion to reach the controls. When Kalpana flew low to the ground, she waved to people below, hoping a child would wave back as she once had.

But Kalpana was destined to fly even higher.
She decided she wanted to go into space!

Even after Kalpana became an American citizen—a requirement for becoming an astronaut in the United States—she always remembered where she had come from. Kalpana was proud of her Indian heritage. She filled the home she shared with JP with Rajasthani decorations, handmade in India. She was a vegetarian and especially liked eating her favorite samosa with imli chutney and sev puri.

Passionate about Bharatanatyam, Kalpana joined
a local Indian dance company.

After she graduated from the University of Colorado, Kalpana and JP moved to California, and she took a job as a research scientist. When the National Aeronautics and Space Administration (NASA) posted an ad for astronaut training, she immediately applied.

BE ONE OF US!

Kalpana met all the qualifications: Test pilot or scientist with a master's degree in a STEM (science, technology, engineering, math) field? *Check*—she had a PhD in aeronautical engineering. Able to pass the rigorous astronaut physical? *Check*—years of hiking, scuba diving, and dancing had kept her in great shape. Between 62 and 75 inches tall? *Check*—but barely, since she was just 62 inches! Related professional experience? *Check*. United States citizen? *Check*.

Yet Kalpana found out it wasn't easy to be picked for astronaut training. Thousands of people applied, but only a few were chosen. NASA turned Kalpana down.

Though disappointed, she didn't give up. Kalpana knew what she wanted. She worked hard in hopes of being chosen the next time. Staying physically active kept her in tip-top condition. She gave presentations and wrote academic papers that highlighted her engineering expertise. Two long years later, when NASA posted another ad, she applied again.

In December 1994, Kalpana answered the phone. Someone from NASA was calling to tell her she was in! But that *still* didn't mean Kalpana's dream of going to space would come true. Not every astronaut is chosen for a mission.

Kalpana and JP packed again and moved to Houston, Texas. Because the training for her astronaut class was delayed, the previous class nicknamed them the "Slugs," after the slow-moving animal. She and the other twenty-two people in her class chose to call themselves a fancier name instead: the "Flying Escargots."

With her fellow trainees, Kalpana learned basic astronaut skills like working in zero gravity, spacewalking, flying T-38 jet planes, and controlling the robotic arm on the space shuttle. After a year of intensive training, Kalpana's class graduated and were now officially astronauts! While waiting to see if she'd get to go to space, Kalpana worked on the ground as a crew representative for technical issues in computers, robotics, and extravehicular activities (EVA).

She didn't have to wait long before NASA chose her to be a mission specialist for STS-87 aboard the *Columbia* space shuttle.

Kalpana and the other five crew members trained together for almost a year, practicing what they would do in emergency situations. To practice EVA maneuvers, they wore spacesuits underwater. They learned to fix delicate equipment while wearing clumsy gloves. Using only materials they might find on board, the crew brainstormed solutions to possible disasters.

On November 19, 1997, STS-87 launched. Each astronaut was allowed to bring a few personal items aboard. Some of the ones Kalpana brought were a Punjab Engineering College banner, T-shirts from her hometown school and the Abhinaya School of Dance, and an Indian Airlines flag—as well as a small rubber slug in honor of her astronaut class.

Each day in space started with a wake-up song selected by a crew member. On their sixth day in space, it was Kalpana's turn. She chose the melodic "Raag Mishra Pilu" played on the sitar by Indian musician Ravi Shankar.

After breakfast and exercising, the day rushed by. Kalpana checked the scientific equipment and recorded data. She ran zero-gravity and vacuum experiments, such as how to make jet engine flames pollute less. As the main operator of the robotic arm, she controlled unloading the fragile satellite. There were even video press conferences from space.

Kalpana never tired of the magnificent view of Earth through the windows. She took breathtaking photos of the world from 170 miles above. When the shuttle orbited over India, she told stories about her country of birth. Perhaps she even waved to the people below.

Against all odds, the little girl from a small town in India had achieved her dream of going into space.

AUTHOR'S NOTE

One of the first things I hung in my daughter Satya's room was a framed illustration of Kalpana Chawla. I wanted Satya to know that like Kalpana, she, too, could reach the stars if she worked hard. Like my parents, Kalpana was an Indian immigrant, someone who left her ancestral home and moved to the United States. Kalpana was brave and hard-working. She wasn't just smart; she was also always learning and trying new things, like traditional Indian dance and how to fly planes. Her life was so inspiring to me because she made opportunities possible for herself, and for those of us who came after her, with her vision and courage.

The quality I admire the most about Kalpana is that she never took no for an answer. Whether it was being told that women don't study aerospace or the fact that it is so difficult to become an astronaut, Kalpana persevered. She knew, in her heart, that she was capable of great things. And so are you.

I hope learning about Kalpana's incredible life makes you ask yourself: What is my dream? What will it take to make my dream a reality? Who will help me as I work to achieve my dream?

Kalpana died far too young, during her second mission to space. But her life had tremendous purpose and her legacy and impact are still felt today. Her life, although short, had so much meaning for her family, for Americans, for Indians, and for kids who dream of going to space themselves. Kalpana's story is really special; it takes a lot of dedication to become a NASA astronaut.

I hope you'll be inspired to share Kalpana's story with someone who may not know about her. Tell them what you admire about her. And show them that, like Kalpana, you are going to chase your own dreams. Then encourage them to chase theirs.

Raakhee Mirchandani

KALPANA CHAWLA'S TIMELINE

MARCH 17, 1962   Kalpana Chawla is born in Karnal, Haryana, India

1982   Receives BS (bachelor of science degree) in aeronautical engineering from Punjab Engineering College

1984   Receives MS (master of science degree) in aeronautical engineering from the University of Texas at Arlington

1988   Receives PhD (doctoral degree) in aeronautical engineering from the University of Colorado Boulder

1988   Hired by MCAT Institute as a research scientist for NASA Ames Research Center

APRIL 10, 1991   Becomes United States citizen

1993   Joins Overset Methods Inc. as vice president and research scientist

DECEMBER 1994   Selected for astronaut training

MARCH 6, 1995   Starts astronaut training in Houston

SPRING 1996   Graduates astronaut training

DECEMBER 7, 1996   Receives call that she has been selected as a mission specialist for *Columbia* space shuttle mission STS-87

NOVEMBER 19, 1997   *Columbia* space shuttle STS-87, her first mission, launches

DECEMBER 5, 1997   STS-87 returns

JANUARY 16, 2003   *Columbia* space shuttle STS-107, her second mission, launches

FEBRUARY 1, 2003   *Columbia* space shuttle is destroyed in the air; Kalpana Chawla dies

HONORS AND RECOGNITIONS

KALPANA'S AWARDS:

Congressional Space Medal of Honor
NASA Space Flight Medal
NASA Distinguished Service Medal
Pravasi Bharatiya Samman Award—given to nonresident Indians for exemplary
   contributions in their field

NAMED AFTER KALPANA (ON EARTH):

Kalpana Chawla Way—Section of 74th Street in Jackson Heights, NY
Kalpana Chawla Hall—University of Texas at Arlington dormitory
Kalpana Chawla Planetarium in Haryana, India
Kalpana Chawla Government Medical College in Karnal, Haryana, India
Kalpana Chawla Award—given to recognize young women scientists

NAMED AFTER KALPANA (IN SPACE):

Chawla Hill—peak on Mars
51826 Kalpanachawla—asteroid that circles between the orbits of Mars
   and Jupiter
Kalpana 1—India's first meteorological satellite

SELECTED RESOURCES

Doordashan National. *Citizen of the Galaxies | Kalpana Chawla | Documentary.*
https://www.youtube.com/watch?v=geHd-G6Vurl. November 6, 2016.

Harrison, Jean-Pierre. *The Edge of Time: The Authoritative Biography of Kalpana
Chawla.* Harrison Publishing, 2011.

Kumar, Abhishek. *Life and Times of Kalpana Chawla.* Prabhat Prakashan, 2017.

Padmanabhan, Anil. *Kalpana Chawla: A Life.* Penguin Random House India, 2003.

Salwi, Dilip M. *Kalpana Chawla: India's First Woman Astronaut.* Rupa & Co., 2016.

LAURIE WALLMARK is an award-winning author who writes biographies of women in STEM, along with fiction. Her books have earned multiple starred trade reviews and received awards such as Best STEM Book and Parents' Choice Gold Medal. Laurie is a former software engineer and computer science professor. She has an MFA in writing and lives in New Jersey.

RAAKHEE MIRCHANDANI is a journalist, children's book author, activist, and mom. Previously a feature writer and columnist for the *New York Post*, a managing editor at the *New York Daily News*, and an associate editor at the *Boston Herald*, Raakhee has had work in *Elle*, *Glamour*, the *Wall Street Journal*, *Redbook*, and *HuffPost*. She was also the editor in chief of *Moneyish*, published by Dow Jones. The daughter of immigrants, Raakhee currently lives in New Jersey.

MAITREYI GHOSH is a multidisciplinary designer specializing in illustration. She illustrated *The ABCs of Virtue*, which was a Best Book Award winner at the American Book Fest in 2021. Maitreyi lives in India.

To my daughters, Kim and Lisa—**LW**

To Liza Fleissig, agent extraordinaire, and Neha Chawla,
for sharing your aunt's legacy with me—**RM**

Text copyright © 2024 Laurie Wallmark and Raakhee Mirchandani
Illustrations by Maitreyi Ghosh, copyright © 2024 Beaming Books

29 28 27 26 25 24 23   1 2 3 4 5 6 7 8 9

Hardcover ISBN: 978-1-5064-8469-3
eBook ISBN: 978-1-5064-8470-9

Library of Congress Cataloging-in-Publication Data

Names: Wallmark, Laurie, author. | Mirchandani, Raakhee, author. | Ghosh,
    Maitreyi, illustrator.
Title: Journey to the stars : Kalpana Chawla, astronaut / by Laurie
    Wallmark and Raakhee Mirchandani ; illustrated by Maitreyi Ghosh.
Description: Minneapolis, MN : Beaming Books, an imprint of 1517 Media,
    2024. | Includes bibliographical references. | Audience: Ages 4-8 |
    Summary: "This inspiring picture book biography follows Kalpana Chawla
    from childhood in India to becoming the first Indian American female
    astronaut, highlighting her dedication, perseverance, and patience"--
    Provided by publisher.
Identifiers: LCCN 2023005319 (print) | LCCN 2023005320 (ebook) | ISBN
    9781506484693 (Hardcover) | ISBN 9781506484709 (eBook)
Subjects: LCSH: Chawla, Kalpana, 1961-2003. | Columbia
    (Spacecraft)--Juvenile literature. | Columbia
    (Spacecraft)--Accidents--Juvenile literature. | Astronauts--United
    States--Biography--Juvenile literature. | Space
    shuttles--Accidents--United States.
Classification: LCC TL789.85.C43 W35 2024 (print) | LCC TL789.85.C43
    (ebook) | DDC 629.450092 [B]--dc23/eng/20230215
LC record available at https://lccn.loc.gov/2023005319
LC ebook record available at https://lccn.loc.gov/2023005320

Beaming Books
PO Box 1209
Minneapolis, MN 55440-1209
Beamingbooks.com

Printed in China.